THE
DUFFER'S
GUIDE TO
BOXING

Mike Gordon

Foreword by Harry Carpenter

COLUMBUS BOOKS   **LONDON**

Other books in the Duffer's series:

Author's note

Many thanks to my wife Maria, Harry Carpenter, Bert Pontremoli, Bryan Parker, Geoff Hopcraft, Linda Setford, Kevin Aves, Johnny Pincham and all at Crawley ABC

First published in Great Britain in 1989 by
Columbus Books Limited
19–23 Ludgate Hill, London EC4M 7PD

Typeset by Poole Typesetting (Wessex) Limited, Bournemouth.

Printed and bound in Great Britain by Hollen Street Press Ltd

ISBN 0 86287 898 5

CONTENTS

Foreword

Boxing is not like other sports. Nobody packs up work on a Friday night and says to his mates, 'That's it, then. Think I'll spend a nice, quiet weekend doing a bit of boxing.'

You are either at it full-time, amateur or pro, or not at all.

You can't relax at boxing as you can with a round of golf. No-one is trying to rearrange your features when you bend over a putt.

In my view, duffers should steer well clear of boxing. Duffers go home with thick ears and bloody noses. So maybe a public health warning should be issued with this book, i.e. Duffers get hurt.

However, if you should happen to get in a fight, remember the rules: (1) Get your whack in first, or (2) Run.

Introduction

Here at last is the guide for those who, when it comes to boxing, know it's their duty to lie down and be counted out. No expense has been spared gathering fighting tips from gyms all over the world.

Now the boxing duffer can discover how to get the knots out of his skipping rope, keep the last of his teeth and look graceful as he falls through the ropes.

Read on for all this and more, but remember - take your gloves off first.

Boxing People

The duffer should soon learn to distinguish the people he meets in boxing, if only to learn which ones he's allowed to punch. The following is a list of people not to punch – which may surprise the duffer who knows they can be more provoking than an opponent.

The club chairman

Given the opportunity, the chairman could talk a sponsorship deal out of the Vatican. Proudly, he'll point out the fading brown photo of the last champion produced by the gym and show you the lads who'll be in the next national squad 'if they grow a couple of inches in the next two weeks'.

The chairman particularly likes to extol the virtues of his club on non-English-speaking tours when his minor embellishments about Las Vegas bookings and his personal role in the making of Mohammed Ali pass largely unnoticed.

The club secretary

She and her fellow ladies on the committee are the stalwarts of every amateur club.

Surrogate mum to all the lads, including the chairman, she's always ready with the first-aid box, a shoulder to cry on and the raffle tickets.

Give her just two days' notice and she'll organize a show in Outer Mongolia with her best boys, providing brand new kit and inside information on all the opposition.

If she ever turned pro, top promoters would choke on their cigars and run for their contracts.

The promoter

Boxing's Mr Fixit. He can draw up a contract faster than a controlling body can say 'vacant title'. His image may be tough and shrewd, but he still has nightmares about Wembley flooding, fighters getting married and television satellites going on the blink.

Boxing couldn't do without promoters. They're the only ones who can remember the names of all the boxing organizations.

The manager

This is a bloke with a great head for percentages and a fist as strong as a fighter's from signing so many deals. He has the eyes of a hawk for reading small print and spotting lipstick traces on his lads from across the gym. Some managers can even stare down the scales at a weigh-in.

Most of all, a manager has a nose for good boxing, which is why duffers don't have managers.

The trainer

One of the friendliest sadists you'll ever meet. Ever so cheery at five o'clock in the morning, he's out with his lads for roadwork, playfully pacing them on his bike, keeping one hand warm on his thermos and one foot out to boot any stragglers.

He's at his happiest announcing a six-week sex ban to ten lads with 150 press-ups and the medicine ball still to go. Duffers should hide in the showers.

The second

This is the man in your corner, cooling you down, wiping your brow, reminding you who you are, etc. Nice enough chap, except that he *will* wear white, which is all right until you realize those little red spots that keep appearing are coming from you.

The cuts man

The pro-boxer's face is like a road to a council workman – *every bleeding crack's got to be filled.* With nothing but a couple of cherry swabs and a drop of adrenalin, a good cuts man could seal the joins on Frankenstein's monster.

14

The referee

Easy to spot, this is the Third Man in the ring, the bossy one not wearing shorts. In fact he dresses more like a waiter, although he never takes orders – he only gives them.

Of course, he's usually a skilled boxing veteran with vast experience and specialist knowledge, except that he can only count up to ten.

The medical man

Always ready to give medicals and provide ring-side attendance, boxing doctors are usually male. A local hospital once sent a female replacement to a tournament but too many bouts were cancelled due to sudden groin strain. You will soon learn ro recognize the doctor. He's the one who keeps popping up between rounds with lots of pretty donor cards in his top pocket and a keen interest in your next of kin.

The judge

Like other boxing officials, the judge needs a licence before he's allowed to keep the score from the ringside. In fact, one judge is said to have lost his licence when it was found he was really awarding points based on looks, personality and vital statistics.

How To Be a Good Fight Fan

It's a well known fact that ladies make the best fight fans. Never setting foot in the ring, they are, of course, the most objective observers of the sport as well as some of the loudest. Naturally, this is especially true when it's their little Johnny getting warned or bashed.

On the next few pages are some tips to assist new fans, male or female, in achieving the same decibel levels of fairminded, critical comment.

1. Get in the drinks
No true fan goes up to the bar again before a tournament interval.

2. Get a good seat
The boxers won't want to strain to listen to your advice and it's not as much fun with binoculars.

3. Try not to spend the rest of your money

This is difficult owing to the number of persuasive, heavily built individuals selling raffle tickets.

5. Assist the referee

Most refs are half blind and need all the help they can get from experts in the crowd.

4. Choose who gets your support

This could be the deciding factor in who wins.

6. Assist the coach

Every good fight fan should be able to convey vital fight instructions, a selection of which is explained here.

Box him
Jab him
Stick it out
Stick your jab at him
Take him
Work, work
One, two, One, two
Mix it

Punch the silly sod

Work, don't wait

Stop hanging about and
punch him.

Downstairs

Punch him lower down.

Shorten 'em up

Stop missing.

Last ten . . .

This indicates the last ten seconds of a round to spur the boxer on to a final assault. Useful encouragement any time from the end of the first minute.

Feet first

Stop standing there, you big plonker.

Cover up

Stop putting your face in front of his gloves.

Scoring

The shaded areas in the accompanying diagrams show the target area of the body and the scoring, knuckle part of the glove.

Unfortunately, these shaded areas cannot be drawn on your opponent so you should do your best to commit them to memory.

Points are scored in this area (of your opponent, not the ref).

Foul (known as a Rabbit Punch, possibly because it makes refs hopping mad).

Foul (not everybody likes devilled kidneys).

Extremely foul.

The Ring

1. Ropes - to rest on.

2. Canvas - to sleep on.

3. Bucket - to spit in.

4. Funnel and tube - from winemaking or enema kits.

5. Stool- pub remnant (try and cut the legs down evenly).

6. Trophies - job lot from Taiwan.

7. Corner post - for judging if you're upright.

8. Neutral corner - to pray in.

9. Blue/red corner - one of two distant, blurred points to return to between rounds. (Your second's voice should guide you to the right one.)

10. Advertising space - for advertiser with long, thin name.

11. More advertising space - in case of TV coverage or low-flying spectators.

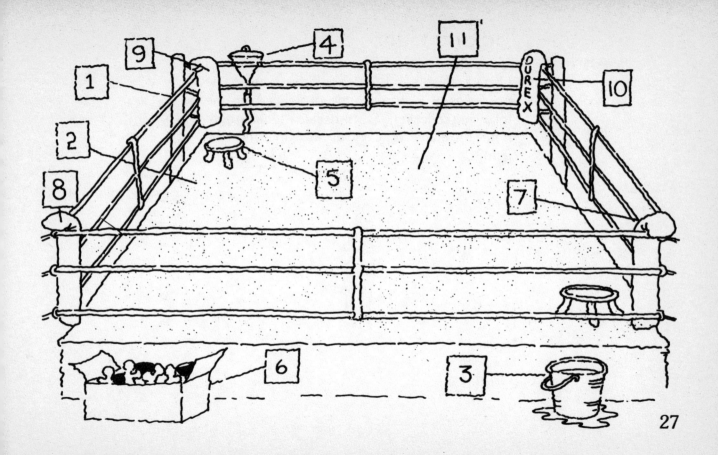

27

Boxing Gear

Naturally, every boxing duffer owns a selection of dark glasses, but he should also ensure he possesses at least a couple of items from the following collection. This is because looking right is half the battle. Why else all those mirrors in the gym?

The headguard

This cosy little contraption not only keeps the brain warm but also thoughtfully leaves room for cauliflowers to sprout either side.

Always remember the protector covers a completely different body part and should on no account be mistaken for a headguard unless you want to be called something extremely rude.

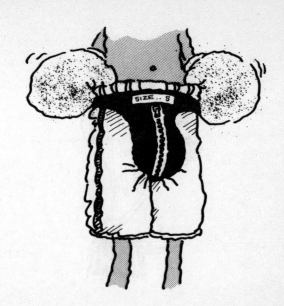

The protector

This vital piece of equipment is used to protect another even more vital piece of equipment. Without it, life could get pretty foul which is why it's known as 'foulproof'. Dented ones make impressive souvenirs even if they do bring back painful memories.

The gumshield

There is no substitute for a proper gumshield. It's a close-fitting personalized item of protection. Orange peel or plastic Dracula sets out of jamboree bags just won't do.

The vest

String vests are no good. It gets too painful when the club name across your chest also sticks to the hairs poking through the little holes.

Dark-coloured ones are good for sparring as they show off the sweat better (or water from a convenient spray), which will impress the trainer. Junior club vests should never be relinquished. They will make you look bigger as a senior.

And of course, all club vests are so smart very few duffers are willing to give them up to become pros.

The trunks

Always keep your boxing trunks in a separate drawer from your flashy underwear. The type of boxer shorts with a large opening in the front is not nearly so elegant in the ring as a pair of proper boxing trunks, even if they have got 'Big Chopper' written in red satin across the opening.

The dressing gown

The idea behind the towelling gown is to look as much like a monk as possible, reflecting the pure life of a boxer in training. Unfortunately for the duffer, this just means those ruddy great sleeves will keep getting in his light ale.

However, every duffer should aspire to a posh, satin ring robe with his name emblazoned on the back. Wearing this over the top will hide all the beer stains and lipstick marks on your towelling gown.

The towel

The main thing is to make sure your corner owns a nice clean white one. If your second has to throw a grubby, old rag of a towel into the ring this won't give anyone a very good impression at all.

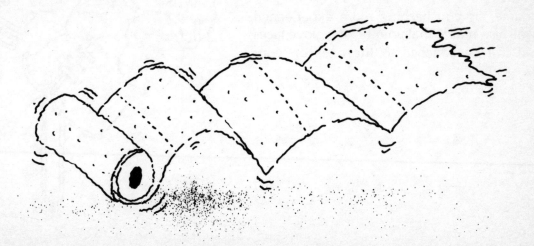

The gloves

At first, you may find it a little difficult deciding which glove goes on which hand. Once you've figured it out, though, the two main advantages to wearing boxing gloves will immediately become apparent:

1. They stop you biting your nails.

2. They prevent you from picking your nose.

Of course, as you become more experienced you will also realize that your boxing glove laces should not be attached to the ones on your boots.

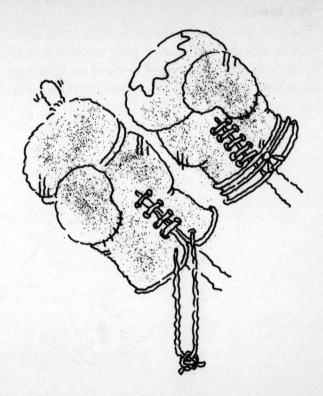

The bandages

It may seem very mean of the officials to allow only certain minimal lengths of protective bandage and tape, especially when what the duffer would really like to wrap round his delicate little mits is a couple of duvets.

What the duffer may not know is that the officials must keep back enough bandage to be able to cover the rest of him once the bout is finished.

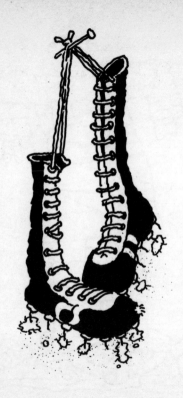

The boots

Boxing boots are usually colourful high-legged affairs. In fact they can be the beginnings of a very good Superman costume. Add a nice pair of red training tights and wear your protector on the outside and you're halfway there.

The Gym

Luxury trimmings at the boxing gym are about as likely as a 'Greasy Nick's' burger van outside a health and country club. Boxing gyms are about blood, sweat and tears and the more there is all over the walls, canvas and manager's office, the better.

Where you spill yours will probably be a choice of one of certain standard variations.

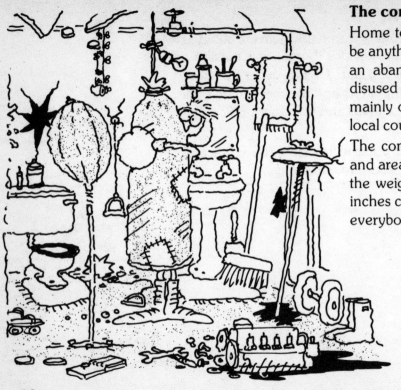

The conversion job

Home to amateur clubs everywhere, this could be anything from a cellar or an allotment shed to an abandoned railway coach on a preferably disused siding. Selection of the site depends mainly on the founder's profession or what the local council hasn't sold off yet.

The committee might have to meet in the loo and areas of dry rot need to be marked out near the weights, but so long as there's at least two inches clearance for the tallest boxer in the ring, everybody's happy.

The purpose-built gymnasium

This is a rare establishment because most boxing gyms are used at least until a demolition order is served. Members at the modern gym try to evoke the past in simple ways such as keeping their founder's urn amongst the trophies.

However, as so many boxers are fresh from the building trade they can't bear to cover up all the new plaster with the usual fight souvenirs.

Duffers go on trial here if they even breathe on the mirrors.

SLUGGER BATES V WILLY THE WIMP

The professional gym

By tradition many of these are strongly connected to licensed premises - usually by floors, walls or ceilings, depending on whether the gym is situated above, below or next to the pub.

Although the beer's off-limits, the atmosphere's just as good in the gym. Historic fight posters cover pre-war cracks, the plumbing is out of the ark and gumshields grin in pickling jars.

Full-time pros pummel away here, and if they don't scare off the duffer the ghosts of fighters past will.

The Equipment

Here, we take you through the principal items used for boxing practice in gyms everywhere. Although these devices are completely lifeless, we should warn you that many have their own attack systems cunningly built in.

Speed ball

The little overhead one that could be mistaken for a black pudding except that it tastes better.

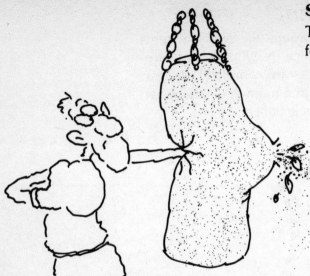

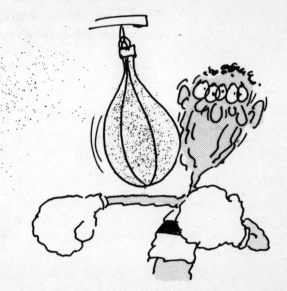

Heavy bag

Good not only for leverage and combinations, but also distraction problems: turn around and it'll give you one heck of a clout from behind.

Medicine ball

Unfortunately named, this heavyweight doesn't cure anything except the novice's tendency to get in its way.

Stand ball

Very good for testing the accuracy and timing of beginners against very thin opponents.

Wall bag
Makes straight-arm punches much more accurate because it hurts so much if you miss.

Floor to ceiling ball
Just in case of very tall opponents.

Punch pads
Held up by the instructor as targets, these are vital coaching aids - they help the coach avoid getting bashed.

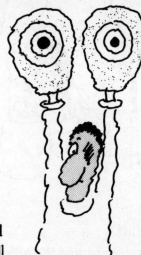

The Punches

Jab, hook, straight right, uppercut, right cross etc. are all words the trainer will expect you to know. What he doesn't tell you is that these are only variations of four much more basic blows. Trainers like to keep things technical. It makes them feel more worthwhile.

The whistler

This one flies at 50 miles an hour, with enough power to flatten an elephant, straight past your opponent's left ear. As it moves to a point approximately six inches behind his head, it generates a high-pitched whistling noise which should be highly intimidating to an opponent. Not recognizing its true value, some boxers refer to this punch as a feint.

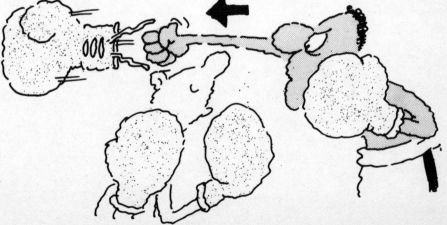

The tickler

This is the uppercut which lands in an armpit or one of many consecutive blows thrown with great effort to the mid-section of an opponent to no effect whatsoever except to make him laugh. In the latter case it is of course a 'rib tickler'.

The cruncher

So called because of the noise it causes bony parts to make. Obviously, a highly damaging punch which could end the fight. This is particularly true when the noise comes from your fingers.

The sledgehammer

This is a scorcher of a blow. Thrown from a textbook stance, hips perfectly pivoted, range spot-on for a powerhouse delivery, it never fails to hit the target, knocking it for six. Everyone will recognize this as the one they throw to the mirror.

Defence

Outlined here are some basic defensive moves grudgingly explained to us between rounds by a veteran trainer. Grudgingly because we ordered doubles when it was his round.

Duck

Bob down, thus ensuring any punch aimed at your chest will now hit your head.

Slip and snap back

This means dodging punches by moving your head sideways or back. It doesn't mean to reply crossly while wearing a petticoat.

53

Cover up

Follow your natural instincts and hide behind your gloves.

Block

Getting a non-target part of your body in the way, such as the shoulder, elbow, left knee, right buttock, big toe, etc.

The Boxer

Whatever his weight, the boxer will have a characteristic approach to the game as in the following examples.

The duffer should learn to assess his opponent and adjust his fight strategy accordingly by informing his second at which round he should have the stretcher ready.

The basher

This is the boxer with about as much technique as a bull terrier with its teeth in a postman. He has one main asset besides his right hand and that's his left hand and his trainer has to tell him which is which.

To a basher the only good opponent is a horizontal opponent. Upright ones really get on his nerves. For each one he knocks out he marks a notch on his protector. Give him a chance and he'd finish the refs off, too.

The artful dodger

This chap combines sparring with ballroom dancing. It takes a big ring to really show off his graceful combination of dainty footwork, enchanting pirouettes and thumping great whacks to his opponent's nose.

Naturally, such skill is lost on the unfortunate opponent. All he knows is that trying to hit this bloke is like trying to swat flies.

The chin man

This guy's chin is his weak point and a very sore one too. He's even been KO-ed catching his chin on his opponent's left hand waving in surrender. However, with a lot of dedication some boxers manage to overcome this vulnerability and can be spotted in restaurants when the cutlery sticks to their lower jaws.

The professor

A dead loss at school but an Einstein in the ring. His brain outperforms the range-finding mathematics of a cruise missile, although he couldn't fill in a tax return if he tried.

He would have made it into the movie-making business, but he failed a Rambo audition because his IQ was too high.

How To Be a Good Pro

There's much more to professional boxing than throwing good punches and wearing gold chains. To become a real champion, the duffer should work on the following tricks of the fighting trade.

The catchphrase

Just a few words are needed here to catch the public's imagination and lift your boxing onto new heights. Just something simple along the lines of 'I am the greatest' or 'Know what I mean?' to tag onto the end of every sentence.

Remember the commentator's name

If you can do this it helps develop a friendly television image which will encourage the advertising and sponsorship deals. Try hard to get the name right because it can also add a little extra polish to your catch phrase as in 'Know what I mean, *Harry*?'

Show a lot of gratitude

This might be hard because it involves remembering more names besides the commentator's. However, the public expects a show of gratitude in front of the cameras even if it does seem daft to thank the manager for taking such a large percentage or the ref for being a one-eyed b*st**d.

Run a pub or a restaurant

It's traditional for boxers to run catering establishments. They're a good second string in case you forget the commentator's name and don't get offered the usual, lucrative sports co-commentator deal.

I Box Because . . .

The authors of this book felt there was a definite need for a lengthy and highly scientific survey of boxers and their complex psychological motivation to thump and be thumped. We are pleased to bring you the results, faithfully recorded as they were on the back of a spare ABA score card.

I can't remember

I like skipping

I never did like by dose

It's in the blood

I can't play the violin

I float like a butterfly

I sting like a bee

Training

Tough, stressful, jarring, draining, excruciating, almost unbearable. So much for the coach, the training's even worse.

A fighter's attitude to the rigours of training will, of course, affect his performance, not to mention his boxing. We invite you to test your attitude on the following pages.

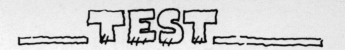

1. A spot of warm-up is suggested. Do you:

a. Start a scientifically balanced session of light jogging and stretching?

b. Bend your knees a couple of times and make an effort to touch your toes?

c. Pull on a woolly jumper and order a double brandy?

73

3. On a target circuit your aim is:

a. Increased stamina and strength.
b. To stay alive.
c. To stay out of sight.

**2. You are trailing on a resistance run.
Do you:**

a. Ignore the pain and step up the pace?
b. Take fifteen minutes' recovery time while you re-tie your boot laces?
c. Remove your leg weights and slip them quietly into the trainer's saddle bag?

5. To improve skipping rhythm and speed do you:

a. Practise very frequently?

b. Chant 'I'm a Little Bubble Car' or similar skipping rhymes?

c. Drive even faster to the pub as you skip alternate training sessions?

4. Weights are:

a. Invaluable training aids.

b. Very heavy.

c. Instruments of torture.

6. You are reprimanded for headbutting while sparring. Do you:

a. Apologize profusely?

b. Claim it was an accident?

c. Use your thumbs next time?

— sorry me 'ed slipped!

7. The coach doubles the number of squat jumps. Do you:

a. Finish them in double time?

b. Pretend you need to go to the loo?

c. Stuff his whistle down his throat?

8. It's a good idea to build up combinations because:

a. They are essential to my attack.

b. I only know two punches.

c. Wearing lots of layers of underwear keeps me warmer.

Score 1 for a); 2 for b); 3 for c)

0-9 What are you doing reading this book?

10-17 The coach is holding you back.

18-24 Well done. This must be your highest ever boxing points total.

The Knockout

(or KO, as in opposite of OK)

This can be a very confusing occurrence, being similar to the effect caused by over-indulgence in alcohol, although the headache which follows a KO isn't nearly so bad.

We are pleased to provide the following detailed description to give duffers a clearer picture of what to expect. It might also stop them claiming it never happened because they don't remember the count or even the contest.

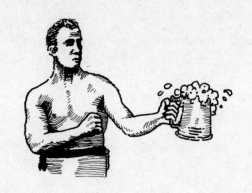